Original title:
When I Was Whole

Copyright © 2024 Swan Charm
All rights reserved.

Author: Sabrina Sarvik
ISBN HARDBACK: 978-9916-89-766-9
ISBN PAPERBACK: 978-9916-89-767-6
ISBN EBOOK: 978-9916-89-768-3

The Redemption of Splintered Whispers

In shadows cast by doubt and fear,
We seek a way for hearts to heal.
With voices soft, we break the night,
In whispered hopes, we find the light.

The pieces lost, we gather round,
In faith, our unity is found.
We share our burdens, dreams, and tears,
Embracing love that calms our fears.

From fractured paths, our spirits rise,
In grace, we learn to see the skies.
Each whispered prayer brings us near,
In harmony, we shed our fear.

With every step, our souls entwine,
In sacred bonds, our hearts align.
The splintered whispers weave a song,
Together, we are ever strong.

Eternal light, our guiding star,
In every wound, we see the scar.
Yet from the pain, new life shall bloom,
In love's embrace, we find our room.

The Quiet Yearning for Unity

Upon the dawn, a soft refrain,
A longing deep, a sweet unknown.
With hearts aligned, we seek to find,
The bonds of grace that intertwine.

In silence shared, our souls ignite,
A gentle flame, a sacred light.
We lift our voices, hopes arise,
In unity, we touch the skies.

Though trials come, we stand as one,
Our spirits soar, the race is run.
In gentle whispers, love does flow,
Together, we embrace the glow.

Each step we take, a path to peace,
In every heart, a sweet release.
With hands held tight, we walk anew,
In quiet faith, our bond is true.

As seasons change, our spirits blend,
In unity, we find the end.
With love's embrace, we soar above,
In every heart, a song of love.

A Biblical Journey of the Heart

In the quiet whispers of night,
Faith walks softly, guiding light.
Through valleys deep, our spirits soar,
In every trial, love's gentle core.

With open hearts, we seek the grace,
In sacred texts, we find our place.
A road of mercy, paths entwined,
In every crossroad, hope aligned.

From ancient scrolls, the truth flows free,
In parables, we learn to be.
With every step, the soul takes flight,
Illumined by the starry night.

In prayerful moments, hearts unite,
Each candle's flame, a beacon bright.
With voices raised, we sing our song,
In harmony, where we belong.

Together, woven in His plan,
In every struggle, we shall stand.
The journey leads us, hand in hand,
By faith, we walk, on holy land.

The Unbroken Circle

In the embrace of a loving kin,
A circle formed, where love begins.
Bound by faith, through thick and thin,
Together we rise, as we walk in.

Through trials faced, we hold on tight,
In darkest hours, we seek the light.
With hearts aligned, we journey forth,
Each spirit shines, revealing worth.

In laughter shared, and tears we shed,
A tapestry of lives we thread.
With hands uplifted, prayers ascend,
The unbroken circle shall not end.

In every story, joy and woe,
Bound by grace, we help each grow.
In every heart, the light still shines,
In all our paths, His love entwines.

Together we stand, forever bold,
In sacred bonds, our hearts consoled.
In unity's grace, we find our way,
The circle unbroken, come what may.

Chronicles of Faith and Wholeness

In pages worn, the stories tell,
Of hearts redeemed, and lives made well.
Through trials faced, and hopes renewed,
In faith we grow, our spirits imbued.

With every chapter, lessons learned,
In flames of love, the heart has burned.
Through darkest nights, and brightest days,
We seek the light, and find our ways.

In whispers soft, the truth unfolds,
In every prayer, His promise holds.
Guided by grace, we rise and stand,
Together bound, in holy band.

In every moment, faith's embrace,
We find our place, in His own grace.
With open hearts, we face our fears,
In love we dwell, beyond the years.

Thus chronicles of faith shall pen,
The stories born of now and then.
In wholeness found, our spirits soar,
In every heart, we are made poor.

The Sacred Echo

In mountains high, His voice resounds,
A sacred echo, across the grounds.
In every heart, the silence breaks,
With tender whispers, his love awakes.

Through forest deep, and river wide,
In nature's song, He will abide.
With every leaf, and bird that sings,
The sacred echo brings us wings.

In storms that rage, He is our guide,
A refuge found, where we confide.
With every prayer, our hearts align,
His gentle peace, a gift divine.

In moments still, we hear His name,
In every spark, ignites the flame.
Through paths unknown, we walk in trust,
In sacred echoes, we are thrust.

So let us rise, with voices clear,
In unity's song, we draw near.
With hearts aflame, we shall proclaim,
The sacred echo, His love our aim.

The Sanctuary of Inner Peace

In the heart, a quiet place,
Where love flows with gentle grace.
In stillness, the spirit sighs,
Underneath the vast, wide skies.

Whispers of hope, softly ring,
In the sanctuary, we cling.
Every breath a sacred trust,
In the light, we find our dust.

With faith, the shadows wane,
As joy becomes our gain.
In unity, we lose our fears,
And find the peace through the years.

Let the calm embrace our soul,
As we surrender and feel whole.
In this haven, storms may cease,
In the sanctuary of peace.

Ode to the Divine Essence

From the depths, a voice does rise,
A hymn that turns toward the skies.
In the beauty of the light,
We find love, pure and bright.

Every heartbeat sings in tune,
Underneath the waning moon.
In the dawn, new life does greet,
In the warmth, our spirits meet.

Eternal grace, a gentle hand,
Guides the soul through this land.
With each moment, we align,
In the essence, we define.

With gratitude, we lift our voice,
In the presence, we rejoice.
Ode to love and wisdom's light,
In the divine, we take flight.

Chalice of Eternal Wholeness

In the chalice, blessings flow,
A sacred drink that helps us grow.
With every sip, a bond we share,
In its fullness, we lay bare.

Reflections of the love divine,
In unity, our souls entwine.
Each drop a journey, sweet and bright,
Guiding us through day and night.

With open hearts, we drink it in,
In its warmth, where love begins.
This chalice holds both pain and grace,
Through every trial, we find place.

Eternal wholeness, we embrace,
In the spirit of His grace.
For within this sacred space,
We find our truest, purest face.

Fragments of the Divine

In the tapestry of life's design,
We gather here, fragments divine.
Each color tells a tale unique,
In the silence, we dare to seek.

Moments shared, like rays of sun,
In the dance, we all are one.
From the ashes, hope will rise,
In the fragments, love never lies.

Each heartbeat, a sacred song,
In the journey, we belong.
Through the trials, we circumcise,
Finding truth in the disguise.

As we weave our lives anew,
In the sheen of morning dew.
Fragments joined, in cosmic flow,
In the light, we come to know.

Heirs of the Light

In the shadowed vale, we rise,
Guided by the starry skies.
With faith as our guiding flame,
In the light, we praise His name.

Boundless love and mercy given,
In our hearts, His truth is driven.
Together, we seek His grace,
Heirs of light in holy space.

Through trials and tribulations, we tread,
By His promise, we are fed.
With every step, we find our way,
In His arms, we long to stay.

Eternal peace surrounds us here,
In our hearts, there is no fear.
For the light is ever bright,
Leading souls through darkest night.

In unity, we lift our voice,
In the Lord, we all rejoice.
Heirs of the light, we stand, we shout,
In His love, there is no doubt.

The Grace of Togetherness

In the bond of spirit, we unite,
Sharing joy, sharing light.
Hands held tight, hearts entwined,
In His grace, we are defined.

Through trials that test our might,
We find strength in shared delight.
Every tear and every smile,
Together, we walk each mile.

In the garden of love, we sow,
With each blessing, we shall grow.
Together, we rise and sing,
In harmony, our praises ring.

Hearts ablaze with holy fire,
In His love, we never tire.
In every laugh, in every prayer,
Together, we find solace there.

The grace we share is a sacred gift,
In each moment, our spirits lift.
Bound by love, through thick and thin,
In togetherness, we begin.

The Restoration of the Soul

In the silence of the night,
Whispers bring our hearts to light.
In reflection, we find the way,
To restore our souls each day.

With every breath, we seek release,
In His presence, we find peace.
From the ashes, we rise anew,
In His love, our spirits grew.

Through storms that rage, we find our calm,
In His mercy, there is balm.
A tapestry of grace unfolds,
The restorative truth it holds.

Each moment, a chance to mend,
In His arms, we transcend.
With each prayer, we draw near,
Restoration whispers, "Do not fear."

With faith as our guiding star,
We journey close, no distance far.
In every heartbeat, we are whole,
Together, in the restoration of the soul.

Meditations on the Eternal

In stillness, we ponder the skies,
Where timeless truths and spirit lies.
In each moment, eternity flows,
A dance of grace, where wisdom grows.

Through ancient words, our hearts ignite,
In whispers soft, we find the light.
With every thought, we touch the divine,
In meditations, our souls align.

The ebb and flow of days and nights,
In His presence, we see the sights.
Here, in silence, He speaks so clear,
In meditative hush, He draws us near.

As the world spins, we stand still,
With open hearts, we seek His will.
In joyful hopes and gentle sighs,
We dwell in love that never dies.

In reflections of the sacred space,
We embrace the eternal grace.
With hearts attuned, in holy quest,
In meditations, we find our rest.

Whispers of the Untouched Heart

In silence, the spirit yearns,
For divine hands to embrace,
Within shadows, the truth burns,
Guiding lost souls to their place.

With every prayer, a soft light,
Unfolds in the depths of despair,
Though darkness may veil the sight,
Hope flickers, a flame in the air.

Songs of the ancients resound,
A melody rich with grace,
In the stillness, love is found,
An unbroken sacred space.

Each whisper is a gentle call,
From the heart of the divine,
In unity, we rise, we fall,
In quiet faith, our souls align.

To the untouched, let us heed,
The blessings that daily unfold,
In the journey, the spirit freed,
In whispers, our truth is told.

The Cradle of Celestial Loss

In twilight's womb, the stars weep,
For the dreams that drift away,
In the silence, the heart must keep,
Memories of a brighter day.

Grief wraps gentle in its cloak,
An embrace for the weary soul,
In sorrow, a soft-spoken stroke,
Mending the cracks that take their toll.

The cradle rocks with echoes sweet,
Of laughter once shared in light,
In every tear, love's heartbeat,
Rests quietly in the night.

From ashes of loss, hope will bloom,
Each petal a promise of grace,
In the depth of the darkest room,
Springs forth the light we embrace.

With reverence for what once was,
We honor the journey we bore,
In celestial loss, there is cause,
For love's everlasting core.

Fragments Reclaimed by Grace

In shattered shards, the light glows,
A testament to what has been,
Through heartache, our spirit flows,
In each fragment, a sacred sheen.

Grace quilts the remnants of our plight,
Stitching wounds with silver thread,
In vulnerability, we find might,
In every tear that we shed.

Through trials, our faith is forged,
A tapestry woven with care,
In courage, our hearts enlarged,
Each battle our spirits declare.

Each fragment tells a tale of love,
Of strength found in the broken ground,
With wings of angels from above,
In grace, our hearts become unbound.

A mosaic crafted by the hand,
Of the One who knows our strife,
In unity, we take a stand,
Embracing the beauty of life.

A Testament of Shattered Light

Through the cracks, the light breaks free,
A testament of hope and pain,
In the broken, we learn to see,
The beauty in life's weary chain.

In every shadow, a promise glows,
Each glimmer, a whisper of grace,
Through the cracks, love's essence flows,
Transforming scars into embrace.

Hope rises like the morning sun,
In the wreckage, we stand anew,
In union, we become as one,
In the shattered, a vision true.

Every challenge, a step we take,
Building bridges from the divide,
In faith, our hearts no longer shake,
In this journey, we will abide.

A testament to the divine light,
Shines brightly through the darkest night,
In our stories, the truth will fight,
For shattered souls, we find our might.

A Tapestry of Belonging

In the weave of sacred threads,
Hearts unite beneath the skies.
Together, we form the fabric,
With love that never dies.

Each whisper echoes in the night,
A song of hope and grace.
Beneath the stars, we find our path,
In this holy place.

Hands extended, spirits rise,
Forging bonds that never part.
In every prayer, a voice is heard,
Binding us heart to heart.

Through trials faced, we walk as one,
With faith our guiding star.
In the shadows, light will shine,
Together, we've come far.

So gather 'round, dear souls of light,
Embrace this sacred truth.
In the tapestry of belonging,
We find our endless youth.

Gathering the Lost Pieces

In the silence of the night,
We gather hope like stars.
Each fragment shines with promise,
Healing our native scars.

With gentle hands, we touch the lost,
Bringing light where shadows dwell.
In the bonds of love, we bind,
Stories only time can tell.

Wounds of sorrow, they may ache,
But in His embrace, we thrive.
Gathering pieces, hearts in prayer,
Knowing we are alive.

Let the warmth of grace descend,
As we search with faithful eyes.
Each shard reflects the sacred truth,
A tapestry of skies.

In unity, we rise anew,
A family through His light.
Together, all lost pieces found,
In His love, our shared might.

The Altar of Remembrance

At the altar, we kneel low,
Bearing burdens, hearts laid bare.
In stillness, whispers of the past,
Linger like a solemn prayer.

Candles flicker, shadows dance,
Stories held in every flame.
Each memory, a cherished gift,
Eternal, never the same.

From silent tears, our strength will rise,
As we honor those we've lost.
In the embrace of love divine,
We count the sacred cost.

With open hearts, we seek the truth,
In every name we speak.
The altar stands as witness here,
To the humble and the meek.

Together, we share this sacred space,
United, forever drawn.
At the altar of remembrance,
We greet each precious dawn.

Seraphim's Comfort

In the wings of seraphim,
Soft voices guide our way.
In shadows, they bring comfort,
Turning night into day.

With radiant light, they beckon,
To the depths of our despair.
Every sorrow, every burden,
They carry with tender care.

Through valleys deep, they walk beside,
Whispering peace to our souls.
In the struggle, we are lifted,
By love that makes us whole.

Their presence feels like summer rain,
Washing wounds, bringing rest.
In the embrace of seraphim,
We find the calm we quest.

So close your eyes, release your fears,
Let the comfort flow in wide.
With seraphim guarding our hearts,
In hope, we shall abide.

The Divine Within the Fractured

In shadows deep, where whispers dwell,
The light within begins to swell.
Each broken shard, a sacred part,
Reflects the pulse of the Creator's heart.

With every fall, a rise anew,
The spirit's strength, in trials true.
From ashes borne, the fire ignites,
Illuminating darkest nights.

Grace flows through cracks, like rivers wide,
Unseen yet felt, where love resides.
In shattered pieces, beauty grows,
A tapestry of grace bestows.

The fractured self, a journey's song,
In unity, we all belong.
The divine dwells in every breath,
From birth to life, through love and death.

So lift your gaze, embrace the whole,
For in each fragment lies the soul.
Together we rise, as one we stand,
In every heart, the Maker's hand.

Threads of Celestial Unity

In the loom of stars, threads intertwine,
Each spark a soul, by design.
The universe hums a sacred tune,
A chorus sung by the sun and moon.

We walk as one, on this fragile earth,
Bound by the threads of love and worth.
In every heartbeat, a shared refrain,
Echoes of joy, and whispers of pain.

The sky unfurls, a tapestry vast,
Uniting the present, future, and past.
In every moment, the divine we chase,
Threads of grace weave time and space.

Let kindness flow, a bridge of light,
Connecting souls in the darkest night.
For in this web, our spirits soar,
In unity's embrace, forevermore.

So gather the threads, and weave them tight,
With love as the fabric, shining bright.
Together we'll rise, and shine our truth,
In this divine dance, we reclaim our youth.

Reflections in Heaven's Mirror

In the mirror clear, our souls we see,
Reflections of love, eternally free.
Each gaze divine, a moment's grace,
In heaven's light, we find our place.

Every tear and smile, a sacred rite,
In the depths of night, we seek the light.
Through trials faced, our faith we hold,
In every heart, a story told.

Grace echoes sweet, in gentle waves,
Through storms we brave, the spirit saves.
In every inch of pain and joy,
Heaven's mirror, life's purest ploy.

So lift your eyes, embrace the shine,
For in each soul, the divine aligns.
In unity found, we rise above,
Reflections of peace, and endless love.

The mirror gleams with truth untold,
In every glance, our hearts unfold.
Together we stand, in bliss we dare,
In heaven's mirror, a love laid bare.

The Heart's Pilgrimage

Upon the path, where shadows tread,
The heart sets forth, in faith we're led.
Each step a prayer, each mile a song,
In the dance of time, we all belong.

Through valleys low and mountains high,
The spirit guides, beneath the sky.
In every trial, a lesson learned,
In every flicker, the fire burned.

With open hands, we share our grace,
In each embrace, a sacred space.
The heart expands, as love unfolds,
In pilgrimage, our truth beholds.

Let every heartbeat resonate,
With visions clear, we elevate.
In unity's embrace, we find our way,
To light the world, come what may.

So journey forth, in hope and light,
With every dawn, we spread our might.
For in the heart's pilgrimage, we see,
The sacred bond of you and me.

Hope Among the Cracked Vessels

In the twilight's gentle sweep,
Where shadows linger, souls do weep.
Cracks adorned with stories old,
Whispered dreams in light untold.

Through the fractures, warmth may rise,
Healing hearts that seek the skies.
In vessels torn, the light does stream,
Each shard reflects a hidden dream.

Among the broken, hope does bloom,
In barren lands, dispelling gloom.
From shattered pieces, strength is found,
In every loss, true love unbound.

With faith, we gather every shard,
Transformed by grace, we are not scarred.
In unity, we stand as one,
With cracks aglow, our journey begun.

The Blessing of a Shattered Existence

In the silence of the night,
Fragments glow with gentle light.
Each wound, a tale of love and loss,
In shattered moments, we find our cross.

Blessed be the heart laid bare,
For in its cracks, we find our prayer.
The pieces scattered, a sacred art,
In every end, a brand new start.

Upon the ruins, faith does stand,
Guided by a tender hand.
In brokenness, we find the way,
To brighter dawns, to hope's display.

From ashes rise, our spirits soar,
In every closing, we open doors.
The shattered essence, pure and free,
Embraced by love, eternally.

Seeker of the Broken Essence

With weary steps, the seeker treads,
Through paths where fading light spreads.
In every crack, a story shows,
Of battles fought and hearts exposed.

Beneath the surface, treasures gleam,
In shattered souls, we weave our dream.
The broken essence sings a song,
Of whispered hopes where we belong.

A journey marked by love's embrace,
Finding strength in each lost trace.
Through ruin's veil, we see the truth,
In fractured forms, eternal youth.

In every scar, a lesson lies,
A testament where beauty cries.
Seeker, lift your eyes to see,
In brokenness, the way to be.

Within the Hallows of Irreparable Grace

In hallowed halls where echoes dwell,
Whispers linger, stories tell.
Of grace that brushes tender wounds,
In broken hearts, a love attunes.

Through stormy nights, a lantern glows,
In shadowed corners, solace flows.
Irreparable, yet beautifully whole,
Restorative grace finds every soul.

With hands extended, we embrace
The fragile threads of time and space.
In every fault, a picture frames,
The sacred dance of love's great claims.

Lift your voice, let gratitude soar,
In every crack, seek and explore.
For in the hallows, life reveals,
The grace in brokenness, it heals.

In the Garden of Grace

In the garden where lily bells ring,
Petals whisper prayers, sweet offerings.
In the stillness, faith blooms bright,
Guided gently by Heaven's light.

Each sigh sings a heavenly prose,
Nourished by love that forever grows.
Beneath the sky, the spirit soars,
In every shadow, His mercy pours.

The brook flows softly, a sacred song,
In its waters, we belong.
Gathering wisdom from ages past,
In this haven, our hearts are cast.

Sunlight filters through emerald leaves,
Each moment in wonder, our heart believes.
Among the blossoms, we find our place,
In every heartbeat, the Garden of Grace.

Where the Spirit Flows

Where the river of life dances wide,
In the depths, our spirits abide.
Waves of mercy, gentle and free,
Carrying hope on the breath of the sea.

Here in the stillness, prayers take flight,
Guided by love, through day and night.
The horizon beckons with promise anew,
Where the Spirit flows, dreams come true.

In the whispering winds, His song we hear,
Echoes of comfort, casting out fear.
Lifted on waves, our troubles cease,
In the current of grace, we find our peace.

With every ripple, truth is revealed,
In His embrace, our wounds are healed.
Journeying forth, hearts open wide,
Where the Spirit flows, we abide.

The Voice of Wholeness

In silence, the voice of wholeness calls,
Awakening hearts, breaking down walls.
Every heartbeat sings with grace,
In the quiet, we seek His face.

The beauty of unity in each soul shines,
Bound by love, the divine aligns.
In shadows dark, His light breaks through,
The voice of wholeness speaks so true.

In trials faced, we find our strength,
Gathering courage, length by length.
For in our struggles, His truth ignites,
The voice of wholeness, a guiding light.

Together as one, we rise and mend,
Hands intertwined, hearts comprehend.
In the symphony of life, we find our song,
The voice of wholeness, where we belong.

Resting in the Divine

Resting in the arms of love so pure,
In His presence, our souls endure.
With gentle grace, He calms the storm,
In quiet surrender, we are reborn.

Through trials faced and paths unclear,
His whispers assure us, always near.
In every tear, a lesson flows,
Resting in the Divine, peace grows.

The light that shines within our doubt,
Brings forth the hope that life's about.
In moments still, our hearts unite,
Resting in the Divine, in pure delight.

Each breath a prayer, humble and bright,
Leading us onward through day and night.
In His embrace, we find the way,
Resting in the Divine, come what may.

In the Footsteps of the Holy Ones

In the stillness of night, we wander,
With hearts bound to the ancient call.
Guided by whispers of the sacred,
We rise above shadows that fall.

In the embrace of love's pure light,
We walk the path laid by the wise.
With faith as our foundation,
We reach for the hallowed skies.

Together we share the burden,
Each step a prayer, each breath a song.
In the grace of the holy presence,
We find where we truly belong.

Through valleys of doubt and despair,
The echoes of prophets ring true.
In the footsteps of the holy ones,
We carry their promise anew.

Bound by the strength of our spirit,
We gather, united as one.
In the footsteps of the holy ones,
Our journey has only begun.

The Circle of Sacred Omen

In the circle of sacred omen,
We gather beneath the starlit dome.
Each heartbeat a rhythmic herald,
A sign that we are never alone.

Whispers of wisdom dance in the air,
A current of truth that ignites our soul.
With every breath, the spirit flows,
Filling the void, making us whole.

In the light of the moon's gentle gaze,
We speak the verses of ages past.
The circle binds us with holy threads,
A tapestry of love that will last.

Knowledge blooms like flowers in spring,
Revealing pathways long concealed.
Together we forge a new beginning,
In sacred moments, our fate is sealed.

Let the circle spin in unity,
A harmony that cannot be broken.
In the circle of sacred omen,
Our hearts speak truths unspoken.

Forgotten Choirs Awaken

In the silence of forgotten hymns,
A melody begins to rise.
With voices that echo through the ages,
We sing our praises to the skies.

From the shadows of history's fold,
Awakening spirits, once asleep.
The choir of souls long silenced,
Calls forth the hearts that yearn to leap.

In the dance of the flickering flame,
We find our strength in unity's glow.
Chords of grace entwine us together,
A symphony of love to bestow.

Each note a prayer, each rhythm a hope,
In the tapestry of divine design.
Forgotten choirs awaken in light,
A promise of healing, pure and fine.

With hearts alight, we join as one,
In the embrace of the sacred sound.
Forgotten choirs awaken anew,
In harmony, our spirits found.

The Resurrection of Spirit

In the dawn of a brand new day,
The spirit rises from the night.
With each breath, renewal whispers,
A promise held in sacred light.

From ashes of sorrow and pain,
New life emerges, bold and free.
The resurrection of spirit beckons,
For all who seek, the heart's decree.

In the garden where hope is sown,
Blossoms bloom, untouched by fear.
Each petal a testament of grace,
A reminder that love is always near.

As the sun kisses the earth below,
Life dances in radiant array.
The resurrection of spirit thrives,
In every moment, come what may.

Let us rise on wings of prayer,
Embracing the journey, hand in hand.
The resurrection of spirit leads,
To a promised, sacred land.

Creating a spirit of wholeness

In the quiet dawn, we rise anew,
A spark of light in every heart.
Mending the broken, binding the torn,
Love's gentle hands play their part.

In every breath, a sacred song,
Unity wrapped in compassion's fold.
Together we stand, unyielding and strong,
In the warmth of truth, we behold.

Through trials faced, we learn to see,
The beauty in our shared strife.
In darkness, we find the strength to be,
In wholeness, we discover life.

As rivers merge in the ocean wide,
So do our souls grow ever near.
In harmony's embrace, we confide,
A spirit of wholeness, pure and clear.

Whispers of the Sacred

Amidst the stillness, whispers call,
Echoes of the sacred, soft and sweet.
In nature's breath, we find it all,
The divine woven in each heartbeat.

In prayer's embrace, the spirit soars,
Words unspoken, yet deeply felt.
Caress of grace through open doors,
In silence, our hearts begin to melt.

Each moment sacred, a thread divine,
Woven through the fabric of our days.
In love's bright light, our souls entwine,
Dance in rhythm, in joy, we praise.

Listen closely to the sacred sound,
The universe whispers, a loving guide.
In every heartbeat, connection found,
Together, in unity, we abide.

In the Embrace of Grace

In the embrace of grace, we find our peace,
Gentle presence, a balm for the soul.
With every falter, our doubts release,
In love's warm arms, we become whole.

Through trials and tears, a light remains,
Guiding us through the darkest night.
In surrender, we break our chains,
Finding strength in the gentle light.

Hope arises, like the morning sun,
Each new day, a canvas bright.
In the dance of life, we are all one,
In grace, our hearts take flight.

Hand in hand, we walk the line,
Together, we rise above the fray.
In the embrace of grace, we shine,
A testament to love's pure way.

Echoes of Eden

In the whispered trees, a story told,
Of creation's breath, of love so pure.
In every heartbeat, a memory old,
Echoes of Eden, forever endure.

Beneath the skies, where dreams take flight,
The gardens bloom with colors bright.
In every shadow, faith ignites,
Guiding our souls through the silent night.

From rivers flowing to mountains tall,
Nature sings of a sacred call.
In every creature, in every thrall,
The echo of Eden connects us all.

With open hearts, we heed the sign,
In unity, love's light we find.
Together we stand, in spirit divine,
Embraced by Eden, our souls aligned.

An Offering of Wholeness

In the garden, where hope blooms bright,
Prayers rise like incense in the night.
Hearts lay bare, in humble grace,
Seeking solace in this sacred place.

Hands entwined beneath the cross,
In surrender, we find our loss.
Each tear a river, each sigh a song,
In His love, we all belong.

From ashes rise the spirit's flame,
In unity, we praise His name.
With every breath, we chant our plea,
For wholeness in our journey to be.

Mountains tremble, valleys sing,
As we gather, our offering.
Together strong, we face the storm,
In faith's embrace, we are reborn.

This is the call, the sacred vow,
To lead with love, to serve right now.
In the silence, we hear His voice,
In our hearts, we make our choice.

The Heart's Reunion

Returning home where shadows fade,
In quiet whispers, hope is made.
From distant shores, our souls did roam,
Yet in His light, we find our home.

With open arms, the heavens greet,
In every heartbeat, love is sweet.
Connection forged in trials faced,
In the tapestry of grace, embraced.

An ancient bond, forever sewn,
In His mercy, we are known.
With every tear, our spirits mend,
In this reunion, we transcend.

Together now, we raise the song,
In His presence, we belong.
For every journey, every tear,
Brings us closer, year by year.

In the stillness, prayers collide,
Hearts ignited, love our guide.
With faith as fuel, we rise anew,
In our reunion, all is true.

Voices of the Redeemed

From the depths, a song ascends,
Broken souls, the Spirit mends.
Voices rise, a chorus clear,
In redemption's light, we have no fear.

Gathered 'round the fire's glow,
Stories shared of pain and woe.
Yet in the darkness, hope ignites,
With every struggle, our faith ignites.

Chains of silence, now released,
In His name, our hearts find peace.
Together in this sacred space,
We lift each other, by His grace.

Lift your hands, let praises soar,
In unity, we're evermore.
Each voice a note, in harmony,
In the choir of eternity.

With every step, we walk in light,
Redeemed souls, burning bright.
In joy and love, we take our stand,
Voices of the redeemed, hand in hand.

A Lament for the Lost

Where are the souls that once were near?
In shadows deep, we shed a tear.
A quiet grief, a heart's ache bare,
For those who wander, lost in despair.

In memories etched, their laughter stays,
Yet silence now fills empty days.
We call their names, echoing pain,
In this lament, our hopes remain.

Oft we question, where did they go?
In searching winds, our spirits blow.
The path is long, with burdens vast,
Yet love entwines the future and past.

With every prayer, we seek their grace,
In every shadow, we find His face.
For even lost, they're not alone,
In heart's embrace, they find their home.

So grieve we must, but not in vain,
For love's bright light will break the chain.
In God's great plan, we trust, we stand,
And hope will guide us, hand in hand.

Homage to the Divine

In the quiet of the night, we pray,
Seeking solace in Your light.
With hearts humble and spirits bright,
We honor You, our guiding sight.

Through the storms that rage and roar,
Your love, our unwavering shore.
In faith, we rise, forevermore,
In worship, our souls do soar.

Each breath a song, each step a dance,
Your presence gives us a second chance.
In Your grace, we find romance,
Bound in love, we wish to enhance.

With voices raised in sweet refrain,
We gather, shedding all our pain.
In Your name, our hearts sustain,
Rejoicing in the love we gain.

Oh Divine, forever we yearn,
With every lesson, in every turn.
Your wisdom, in our spirits, churn,
In trust and hope, together we learn.

The Flame of Restoration

In shadows deep, Your light appears,
A beacon bright, dispelling fears.
With every touch, my heart it steers,
Towards the path where love adheres.

A flame ignites within my soul,
Transforming pain, making me whole.
With each embrace, I feel the toll,
Of love divine that makes me whole.

Through trials faced, my spirit grows,
In darkness, still Your presence glows.
With faith ignited, hope bestows,
A strength that through my being flows.

O gentle flame, consume my doubt,
In Your embrace, I dance about.
With gratitude, my heart will shout,
In sacred love, I am devout.

For in Your warmth, my fears recede,
You are the light, the heart's pure seed.
Restoration's gift, through love we heed,
In every moment, Your grace I need.

Journey through the Light

With every step upon this way,
I feel the warmth of dawn's bright ray.
Through valleys low and mountains gray,
Your presence guides me day by day.

In whispers soft, You call my name,
Transforming fear into holy flame.
Through trials faced, I yield my claim,
In every struggle, You remain.

Through winding roads, I tread with grace,
In every heartbeat, I seek Your face.
Your love, a constant, warm embrace,
Through every trial, my soul finds space.

The light, it dances all around,
In valleys low, on hallowed ground.
With faith and love, my heart is bound,
In every moment, You are found.

So let me walk with You in trust,
In every stride, surrender must.
In light divine, my spirit gusts,
In You, O Lord, my heart is thrust.

A Parable of Healing

In stories told beneath the sky,
Of broken hearts that sought to fly.
With gentle hands, You draw us nigh,
In love's embrace, our fears all die.

From ashes rise, the phoenix born,
In every tear, a promise sworn.
Through trials harsh and nights so worn,
A testament to hope reborn.

The rivers flow with grace untold,
Restoring wounds, making hearts bold.
In every lesson, love unfolds,
In sacred whispers, truth behold.

O healer of the weary soul,
In darkness deep, You make me whole.
With every word, You play the role,
Of gentle hands that softly console.

Let every heart become the seed,
Of hope and love, that we may lead.
In every story, hearts proceed,
To healing paths, where grace is freed.

The Harmony of Creation

In the stillness of dawn's embrace,
The whispers of life begin to flow.
Each creature dances, each tree sways,
In the symphony of God's grand show.

Mountains rise and valleys bow,
Rivers sing through the land they seek.
Stars twinkle in the nightly vow,
In this creation, we find our peace.

The sun ignites the morning glow,
As flowers bloom with colors bright.
Every heartbeat, a sacred echo,
In the arms of the divine light.

Nature cradles us with care,
The wind carries our silent prayers.
In harmony, our souls repair,
United in love, our lives we share.

Let us roam through fields of grace,
With gratitude upon our lips.
For in each moment, we can trace,
The heart of God in every glimpse.

The Bridge of Belonging

Across the river of despair,
A bridge of hope begins to rise.
Each step forward is a prayer,
With every heartbeat, love survives.

In unity, our hands entwine,
Through trials faced, we learn to fly.
Together, we are the divine,
With faith that lifts us to the sky.

Voices merge in joyful song,
In fellowship, we stand as one.
With hearts ablaze, we journey long,
For in each other, we have won.

The path may twist, the road may bend,
Yet through the storm, we hold on tight.
For every wound shall find its mend,
When love's embrace is our guiding light.

In every moment, we proclaim,
Our bond as strong as sacred ties.
In the tapestry of His name,
We weave a home, where true love lies.

A Light in Dissonance

When shadows loom and voices wail,
A flicker shines amidst the gloom.
In every trial, we shall prevail,
For love will pierce the darkest room.

In discord, grace begins to bloom,
A melody softens hardened hearts.
Through every loss, we find our tune,
For from the pain, a new hope starts.

Faith ignites the dreary night,
A beacon guiding weary souls.
Each storm may roar with all its might,
Yet love sustains us, makes us whole.

In silence, whispers of the past,
Remind us of the journey's worth.
For through the struggle, light is cast,
In unison, we dance the earth.

A testament to strength within,
As we rise with spirits high.
In every fracture, we begin,
To find the beauty in the cry.

The Graceful Path

With each step upon this road,
We walk with faith, hand in hand.
In every burden, love's bestowed,
Guided by the great divine plan.

The winds may change, the seasons shift,
Yet through it all, our hearts remain.
In every trial, we find a gift,
A chance to grow, to love, to gain.

The mountains high, the valleys low,
Are but reflections of our soul.
In every challenge, we shall know,
That grace mends us, and makes us whole.

In quiet moments, wisdom speaks,
Through tender whispers of the light.
With every heartbeat, hope it seeks,
To guide us through the endless night.

So let us walk this path of grace,
With gratitude for every stride.
In unity, we find our place,
Forever blessed, always allied.

The Covenant of Lost Wholeness

In shadows deep, the silence breathes,
A whisper lingers, time reweaves.
The fragments yearn for unity's light,
In fractured hearts, hope takes flight.

The promise forged in sacred night,
Each tear a token, each wrong a right.
We seek the bond of ages past,
In love's embrace, our souls held fast.

Through trials faced, we rise anew,
With hands outstretched, the lost pursue.
In every sorrow, grace descends,
A healing touch that never ends.

Together we weave the fabric whole,
In brokenness, we find our role.
The covenant shines with each shared breath,
A testament beyond our death.

For in the dark, the light reveals,
The thread of faith that gently heals.
In every fracture, love's design,
A path to wholeness, yours and mine.

Prayers Among the Fractured

We gather here in sacred space,
In whispered hopes, we seek His grace.
Among the lost, our voices rise,
In solemn prayer beneath the skies.

Each breath a longing, each sigh a plea,
To mend the bonds, to set us free.
In the chaos, a heart still beats,
In the silence, our spirit meets.

Among the shattered, faith remains,
In every struggle, love sustains.
We lift our hearts as offerings true,
A tapestry of me and you.

In broken places, grace is found,
Through every tear, our hope unbound.
We stand together, hand in hand,
In prayer we rise, together we stand.

So let the healing waters flow,
Through every crack, let kindness grow.
Among the fractured, we find our song,
In unity's chorus, we all belong.

Tracing Lines of Divine Remembrance

In moments pause, we trace the line,
Of sacred whispers, the love divine.
Each memory like stars afire,
Guides our souls through trials dire.

We search the echoes of His grace,
In every shadow, we find His face.
Each step a dance in rhythm's flow,
In divine presence, our spirits grow.

Through ancient paths, our footsteps tread,
In every heart, the light is spread.
We bind our wounds with threads of trust,
In the soil of faith, we rise from dust.

The lines we trace begin to blend,
A sacred map that knows no end.
For in His arms, we find the way,
In every dawn, the hope of day.

In remembrance deep, the love remains,
In every heartbeat, joy sustains.
We celebrate the ties that bind,
In sacred moments, we are aligned.

The Sacred Art of Becoming Whole

In every crack, the light breaks through,
In broken pieces, the heart finds view.
With every step on this holy ground,
A sacred art in love profound.

Each fragment tells a story vast,
Of trials faced and shadows cast.
We gather strength from wounds adorned,
In healing grace, our spirits warmed.

In the dance of life, we learn to bend,
To weave the light, on love depend.
In every sorrow, joy is born,
A symphony of the lost reborn.

Through sacred rituals, we align,
In shared communion, the stars combine.
We lift our voices, gratitude flows,
In every heartbeat, the spirit knows.

As days unfold, we're shaped anew,
In the canvas of creation's dew.
The sacred art of becoming whole,
Embracing life, entwining soul.

Dancing with Angels

In the twilight glow of grace,
Angels gather, hearts embrace.
With every step, we find our way,
In sacred rhythm, night and day.

Whispers soft as morning dew,
They guide us gently, ever true.
With wings of light, they soar so high,
In joyful dance, we join the sky.

Through trials faced, we still rejoice,
With every heartbeat, joy's sweet voice.
Together, we are woven tight,
In love's embrace, our spirits light.

In this moment, we are free,
Finding strength in unity.
As angels lead, our souls aligned,
In endless grace, our hearts combined.

So let us twirl in trust divine,
With heavenly hosts, our spirits shine.
In every step, we feel the praise,
As we dance through all our days.

Mandala of the Spirit

In every corner of the earth,
Lies the sacred dance of birth.
Patterns formed by hands and hearts,
Whirling flames where spirit starts.

Colors bright, a canvas wide,
Showing paths with love as guide.
In unity, we sketch our fate,
A mandala, we weave, create.

Moments blend in sacred space,
Each breath taken, a soft embrace.
The universe, our tapestry,
With threads of light from you and me.

Round and round, the cycles flow,
In every joy, in every woe.
Together, we are one, we're whole,
The mandala of the soul.

So let us paint with every prayer,
Creating beauty everywhere.
In spirit's dance, we find our truth,
A timeless bond, an endless youth.

The Call to Wholeness

Hear the whispers in the night,
Calling souls to seek the light.
In the stillness, voices blend,
A gentle call, our hearts extend.

Each longing leads us to the flame,
A path of love, we must reclaim.
For wholeness dwells in unity,
In every bond, we find divinity.

Releasing fears, we stand as one,
Together shining like the sun.
In the embrace of sacred trust,
We rise anew, as all souls must.

So heed the call, let love unfold,
In every story, brave and bold.
We gather now, our spirits twine,
In wholeness sweet, a love divine.

Together we shall walk this way,
United hearts, come what may.
As we journey on, hand in hand,
In the garden of the promised land.

Beneath the Divine Canopy

Underneath the stars so bright,
We gather here, hearts filled with light.
Beneath the canopy of grace,
In sacred stillness, we find our place.

The universe sings, a soothing hymn,
A promise made, a love that's brimmed.
In every breath, divinity flows,
The purest love, in silence grows.

As shadows dance and moonlight glows,
Our spirits rise where blessings flow.
In every heartbeat, the world aligns,
A sacred bond that forever shines.

Together we stand, hands held high,
In this moment, we touch the sky.
Under the stars, our dreams take flight,
Beneath the canopy of night.

So let us cherish what we've found,
In the stillness, love abounds.
With open hearts, we stand as one,
Beneath the divine, 'til night is done.

Embracing the Divine Division

In shadows cast by sacred light,
We ponder paths of wrong and right.
The heart divides, yet seeks to bind,
In every soul, a quest designed.

Oh, how we falter, yet we rise,
With whispered prayers, we touch the skies.
Each fracture sings a holy song,
In unity, we still belong.

A morning star shines through the pain,
In fractured mirrors, truth remains.
Our differences, a sacred thread,
In every word, a light is spread.

Learn to embrace the bitter strife,
For in our discord, there is life.
To seek the peace, we must believe,
In every heart, a chance to cleave.

As souls entwined, we walk the road,
With every burden, share the load.
Embracing divisions, we draw near,
In sacred love, there is no fear.

Reverent Echoes of Innocence

In morning dew where children play,
The world awakens, bright as day.
With eyes like stars and hearts that dream,
In innocence, pure spirits gleam.

A gentle breeze, a fleeting thought,
In every smile, a lesson taught.
The laughter rings like silver chimes,
In reverence, we cherish times.

O gentle souls with love so pure,
In every hug, the heart's allure.
To see the world through childlike grace,
Is to embrace the sacred space.

With every tear and joyful cheer,
The echoes whisper, always near.
Embrace the light that dances free,
In every child, the divine we see.

For innocence holds a sacred truth,
In every eye, the spark of youth.
Oh, let us honor and protect,
The reverent echoes we reflect.

The Garden of Unfurling Sorrows

In twilight's glow, the petals fall,
Each whispered woe, a sacred call.
A garden grows where sorrows blend,
In silence, broken hearts can mend.

The shadows stretch, embracing pain,
In every tear, a soft refrain.
With roots entwined in sorrowed earth,
We find the seeds of silent worth.

From thorns, the blooms of life emerge,
In every wound, a chance to surge.
Transform the ache into a song,
In the garden, we all belong.

With every storm, the flowers sway,
In beauty, they will find their way.
The fragrance of our deepest grief,
Brings forth the hope, a sweet relief.

So linger here in sacred space,
Among the blooms, we're shown His grace.
For in our sorrows, love does grow,
A garden vast, where blessings flow.

Pilgrimage of the Splintered Soul

Upon the path where shadows dwell,
The splintered soul begins to swell.
With every step, a heavy heart,
Yet still we seek to make a start.

In search of light through darkest night,
The journey calls with whispered might.
Each fragment calls from deep within,
To pave the way, let healing begin.

With open arms, we face our strife,
In every sorrow, lies new life.
Through valleys low and mountains high,
The spirit soars beyond the sky.

United shards of broken dreams,
In every tear, a love redeems.
The pilgrimage, a sacred quest,
To find in pain, life's truest rest.

So walk with grace, though splintered be,
In every step, the soul is free.
For in the journey, we shall find,
A path where heart and spirit bind.

Testament of Wholeness

In the light, we find our way,
Guided by grace, we shall stay.
Each soul a thread in the grand design,
Together we rise, as stars align.

From the ashes, a new life grows,
In unity's strength, the spirit flows.
Seek the truth in the quiet night,
Embrace the dawn, let love ignite.

In every heart, a sacred spark,
Kindled in joy, it brightens the dark.
Journey together, hand in hand,
Fulfilling dreams, in faith we stand.

Whispers of wisdom fill the air,
Voices of hope, an answered prayer.
In the silence, His message clear,
We sing together, casting out fear.

Life is a circle, eternally spun,
Each moment cherished, the race we run.
In the tapestry, our stories weave,
In love and trust, we shall believe.

Enlightened Footprints

Upon this path, where blessings flow,
Each step we take, His love will show.
With every breath, a purpose born,
In the light of dawn, our spirits adorn.

Guided by stars in the evening sky,
We weave our dreams, together we fly.
From the earth's embrace, wisdom unfolds,
In our hearts, a truth that holds.

Through valleys deep and mountains high,
In faith we wander, never shy.
Every tear shed, a lesson learned,
In the fires of faith, our souls shall burn.

We walk in love, on sacred ground,
In the dance of life, our joy is found.
Step by step, with hearts so pure,
Boundless grace in hope we endure.

With open arms, we greet the day,
In the morning light, we shall pray.
Eternal footsteps, through time they tread,
In every heart, His love is spread.

The Harmony of Existence

In the stillness, the world unfolds,
A symphony of stories told.
In every heartbeat, a rhythm flows,
Life's sweet melody, as the spirit grows.

The trees whisper secrets to the breeze,
Nature sings songs that put us at ease.
In the cosmos vast, we find our place,
In the dance of life, we seek His grace.

Together we rise, like morning light,
In the embrace of love, we ignite.
Every color, every hue,
A testament that life is true.

Through trials faced and losses borne,
We discover hope, rebirth is sworn.
In our unity, the truth we find,
In the heart's harmony, we're intertwined.

In the laughter shared and tears we shed,
In the simple things, our spirits are fed.
The harmony of existence sings,
Immortal love, to which our heart clings.

Silent Songs of the Heart

In the quiet whispers, the soul speaks,
Soft melodies that love uniquely seeks.
In the shadows cast by the fading light,
A symphony of faith ignites the night.

With every breath, a note of grace,
In the silence, we find our place.
Songs of the heart, so tender and true,
Echo through time in the love we pursue.

Through valleys of doubt, we softly tread,
In the language of love, we're forever led.
Each heartbeat a song, a sacred refrain,
In the silence of souls, joy conquers pain.

In the pauses, the magic lives,
In giving of self, the heart forgives.
Through the storms that may tear us apart,
We find our way back to love's pure heart.

So let the silent songs embrace our days,
In gratitude, we offer our praise.
For in the quiet, true strength shall rise,
In the sacred silence, love never dies.

The Altar of Forgotten Dreams

In shadows deep, dreams lie forgotten,
Whispers of hope among the dust.
Hands clasped in prayer, hearts once wrought,
Seeking solace where faith is just.

Echoes of laughter in silent halls,
Visions of glory, now torn apart.
The altar stands, weary and frail,
Yet still it cradles the yearning heart.

Each tear that falls is a seed of grace,
A promise bound in the sacred night.
From ashes rise, the dreams once lost,
Illuminated by eternal light.

In the stillness, a gentle breath,
Breath of the past, the future's seed.
With every prayer, a step towards truth,
In the heart's deep well, we find the need.

So gather round, O souls in search,
The altar awaits, our hopes it saves.
In unity, with faith's embrace,
We rise anew from our shadowed graves.

Hymn to the Once Complete

O melody of days gone by,
When hearts, in rhythm, beat as one.
In sacred harmonies we sang,
A hymn to life, with joy begun.

Yet, silence fell, and chords did break,
A symphony lost in shifting time.
In minor keys, our voices fell,
And echoes linger in whispered rhyme.

Remember us, O song of yore,
Your splendor shines in memory's glow.
With every note, restart the flame,
And guide us through the ebb and flow.

O blend our dreams, let them resound,
In unity, we shall not wane.
From ashes rise, in grace, reborn,
Together in this sacred refrain.

In fervent prayer, we seek the light,
To heal the scars, the fractured part.
With joyful hearts, we sing once more,
A hymn to the sacredness of the heart.

Beneath the Weeping Willow

Beneath the willow, shadows dance,
A tranquil place where spirits dwell.
With every breeze, a soft romance,
   Whispers of love in nature's swell.

The branches weep, as dreams take flight,
   In every tear, a tale of grace.
We find our peace in the soft twilight,
In the willow's arms, a warm embrace.

O ancient tree, with roots so deep,
   In your shade, the weary rest.
Memories linger, secrets keep,
With every sigh, the soul is blessed.

Here in the quiet, we draw near,
To listen close to the heart's soft song.
In gentle stillness, we conquer fear,
In the willow's wisdom, we belong.

As dusk descends, the world slows down,
   Beneath the stars, our spirits rise.
In nature's cradle, hearts unbound,
Together we bask in love's reprise.

In the Embrace of Sacred Silence

In silence deep, a world awaits,
Where echoes fade into the night.
In the stillness, the spirit operates,
Finding solace in the hidden light.

Each moment breathes a sacred truth,
Revealing whispers, soft as prayer.
As we surrender, the heart finds youth,
In tranquil depths, we lay bare.

Amongst the stars, in cosmic calm,
Infinity wraps us in its song.
In the embrace, we find our balm,
That heals the wounds where we belong.

O sacred silence, guide our way,
In your valleys, peace we find.
With every heartbeat, we softly pray,
In your arms, our souls entwined.

So let us dwell, in this divine,
In the quietude, our spirits rise.
Together, in grace, our hearts align,
In the embrace of the endless skies.

Lamentations of a Splintered Soul

In shadows deep, my spirit cries,
A fractured heart beneath dark skies.
Echoes of sorrow, whispering pain,
Yearning for solace, love's sweet reign.

As I wander through dusk's embrace,
Seeking refuge, a sacred place.
Hope flickers dim, yet still it glows,
In the silence where anguish flows.

Lost in a world where shadows dwell,
Each tear, a story I long to tell.
Fragments of trust, scattered like dust,
In the arms of despair, I place my trust.

Yet through the ache, a glimmer bright,
A promise held in the still of night.
Broken wings yearn to ascend,
To find redemption, to mend, to bend.

So I rise from the depths of my plight,
With whispers of faith to guide my fight.
Though splintered, still whole, my soul shall sing,
For in every crack, a new hope springs.

The Light That Kindled in Ruins

In the ashes where dreams lay bare,
A light emerges, fragile but rare.
Hope ignites where darkness reigned,
A flicker, a spark, love unchained.

From crumbled stones, a voice will rise,
Resounding truths beneath gray skies.
Each heartbeat echoes, the past, the pain,
Yet through the ruins, hope does remain.

Through trials faced and battles fought,
We search for meaning, lessons taught.
In every tear, a seed of grace,
The light that shines will find its place.

With open hearts, we gather near,
Embracing the love that conquers fear.
From despair's grip, we shall ascend,
For all that's broken can still mend.

In the light that kindled from despair,
We find each other, united in prayer.
For even in ruins, hope can bloom,
A reminder that love will resume.

Echoes of Harmony in Dissonance

When chaos reigns and silence falls,
Harmony whispers through the walls.
In discordant notes, a truth shall show,
Forgive the hurts, let the healing flow.

In every storm, a melody plays,
A song of hope in turbulent days.
Every heartbeat, a rhythmic dance,
Embracing shadows in love's expanse.

Though life may bend, it will not break,
In sorrow's grip, our spirits wake.
For every loss, a gain awaits,
In echoes resound, the heart relates.

Together we rise, from fractures mend,
United in faith, we learn to bend.
Beyond the noise, love's gentle grace,
In harmony found, we find our place.

So let us sing amidst the strife,
For in dissonance, we weave our life.
Each note a prayer, each voice a key,
In echoes of love, we long to be free.

The Risen Bones of Forgotten Faith

From depths below, where whispers fade,
The bones of faith in shadows laid.
Yet, in the silence, a breath anew,
A promise stirs, and hope breaks through.

With shattered dreams, we stand once more,
To reclaim the path that faith wore.
In every crack, a story lies,
Waiting for hearts to rise and fly.

Though time may struggle, and doubt may creep,
In the echoes of silence, our spirits leap.
For every fracture, a lesson learned,
From ashes of sorrow, our hearts have turned.

So we gather the bones, in reverence stand,
With hands entwined, uplifted, and planned.
For the past may haunt, but we hold the key,
In the dawn of faith, we choose to be free.

Together we rise, our voices sing,
From forgotten depths, new life we bring.
In the light of grace, our bones shall dance,
Embracing the faith of a second chance.

Rebirth in the Divine Embrace

In shadows deep, we seek the light,
A whisper calls, to set us right.
From ashes born, we rise anew,
To dance in grace, our spirits true.

Heaven's grace, a gentle rain,
Washes away our earthly pain.
In love's embrace, we find our peace,
And in the joy, our fears release.

The sacred flame ignites our hearts,
With every breath, the soul imparts.
In unity, our voices soar,
As one we stand, forevermore.

Renewed each day, in faith we bloom,
With open arms, we cast off gloom.
In every trial, divine we see,
Together bound, forever free.

The Covenant of Souls

In the silence where spirits meet,
A sacred bond, strong and sweet.
Whispers echo in the night,
Binding hearts in love's pure light.

Promises made in sacred trust,
In every soul, a hint of must.
We gather here, our hopes aligned,
In this union, our fates entwined.

As seasons change, our spirits grow,
Through joy and sorrow, deep embrace flow.
The path we walk, in faith we tread,
A trail of love, where angels led.

Infinite grace, the guiding star,
In every struggle, near or far.
With open hearts, we dare to dream,
In this sacred space, we share our gleam.

Together we rise, hand in hand,
Carving hope through this promised land.
An eternal dance, a cosmic role,
Forever bound, the covenant of souls.

In Search of Sanctuary

In weary hearts, we seek a place,
A haven found in love's embrace.
Through trials faced, and shadows cast,
A refuge built to hold us fast.

In prayers whispered to the skies,
Each tear a token, sweet and wise.
The light within, a guiding flame,
In every heart, we know the name.

The walls of faith, our strong defense,
In sacred ground, we find our sense.
Though storms may rage, we stand as one,
Our spirits dance beneath the sun.

We gather 'round in love's embrace,
No judgment found in this safe space.
Together bound, we rise anew,
In search of peace, we've found what's true.

Through darkest nights, our hope will soar,
In search of sanctuary, ever more.
With every heartbeat, we proclaim,
Together here, we lift His name.

The Mosaic of Creation

In vibrant hues, the world unfolds,
A tapestry of life retold.
From mountain peaks to oceans wide,
In every breath, the spark resides.

Stars align in cosmic dance,
Each twinkling glow, a sacred chance.
The universe, a grand design,
In perfect harmony, we align.

Every creature, a note in song,
In unity, we all belong.
The laughter shared, the tears we cry,
In love's embrace, we live and die.

The hands that paint the skies so blue,
Are ours to cherish, to renew.
In every dawn, a chance to see,
The glorious dance of you and me.

With open eyes, we journey forth,
Embracing all, for what it's worth.
The mosaic stands, forever bright,
In creation's arms, we find our light.

Journeys Through the Fractured Light

In shadows cast by broken dreams,
We wander paths of fractured light.
Each step, a testament of faith,
Resilient hearts draw ever bright.

Through valleys low and mountains high,
The spirit soars like doves in flight.
Amidst the chaos, hope ignites,
Our souls unite to seek what's right.

Beneath the stars, we trace our tales,
In whispers shared with night's embrace.
For every trial, a lesson learned,
We rise anew in love's warm grace.

Though storms may come and shadows loom,
In sacred silence, we find peace.
Together we shall face the gloom,
With every heartbeat, doubts release.

Our journeys wend through sacred roads,
With trust as compass, hearts aligned.
Together we bear burdens light,
In fractured light, our paths defined.

Odes to Vanished Integrity

Once proud with honor, now we mourn,
The echoes of integrity lost.
In fleeting moments, we reflect,
The cost of truth, a heavy frost.

With voices raised, we seek to heal,
A world where light meets darkest fears.
In unity, our song shall rise,
To gather strength through clouded tears.

In quiet chambers of the heart,
We cradle whispers of the past.
With every step, let love prevail,
In odes of hope that hold us fast.

For every promise, gently spoken,
We yearn to reignite the flame.
With courage found in honest roots,
We write anew integrity's name.

A tapestry of faith we weave,
Each thread a story, strand of light.
United hearts, we rise again,
As beacons through the longest night.

The Soul's Distant Horizon

Across the sea of dreams untold,
The horizon calls with gentle grace.
In search of meaning, we embark,
Our souls entwined in sacred space.

With every wave that kisses sand,
We gather visions, hopes, and fears.
The distant stars, they guide our way,
Illuminating paths through years.

In quiet moments, wisdom speaks,
Revealing truths from deep within.
Though journeys may at times divide,
Our spirits dance to love's sweet hymn.

Through valleys vast and mountains steep,
We trace the lines of destiny.
In unity, we rise above,
With faith to mark each memory.

The soul's horizon beckons bright,
In every heartbeat, joy and strife.
Together, let us seek and find,
The sacred dressings of this life.

The Divine Dance of Reassembly

In fragments cast by fate's cruel hand,
We gather pieces, lost yet whole.
With tender grace, we weave anew,
The tapestry of one shared soul.

Each twist and turn, a sacred rite,
In every sorrow, laughter's spark.
Through trials faced with hearts ablaze,
We dance in light amidst the dark.

With every step, our spirits merge,
In holy movement, bonds refined.
Together we embrace the pain,
To find the love that's intertwined.

In circles drawn from ancient songs,
We find our truth in rhythms strange.
The divine call within us swells,
A symphony of life, we change.

So let us twirl in faith's embrace,
As hands unite to mend the seams.
In this divine dance, we reclaim,
The light of hope, our waking dreams.

Pilgrimage to the Heart

In quiet steps I wander, seeking grace,
Through valleys deep, and shadows that embrace.
Each heartbeat whispers, love's eternal call,
To tread the sacred path, where spirits fall.

The dawn unfolds a promise, soft and bright,
As morning dew reflects the dawning light.
With every breath, a prayer dances free,
Guiding my soul towards the holy sea.

In temples of the earth, I find repose,
Among the ancient trees, where wisdom grows.
The whispers of the ages fill the air,
Inviting me to linger, to be bare.

With faith as my companion, I ascend,
Each step a testament, each breath a bend.
In pilgrimage I gather, dreams untold,
In the heart's deep chamber, truths unfold.

At journey's end, I find a sacred space,
The love within, a boundless, warm embrace.
My heart, a vessel, holds the tales of yore,
In pilgrimage to Self, I am restored.

Solace in the Sacred

In stillness lies the beauty of the night,
Where shadows dance beneath the moon's soft light.
A sacred whisper floats upon the breeze,
Leading hearts to find their inner peace.

The stars align, a map of dreams anew,
Each glimmer speaks of love, so pure, so true.
Within the silence, souls begin to mend,
Finding solace in the depths of the blend.

A river flows with currents of the past,
Where waters echo stories that will last.
In sacred moments, wisdom does reside,
As hearts entwine, with spirit as their guide.

The temple of the soul, a radiant space,
Illuminating shadows with divine grace.
In prayerful hearts, the world finds its song,
In solace found, we know where we belong.

As dawn breaks gently, blessings fill the air,
With every breath, the infinite's love share.
In sacred rhythm, life begins to flow,
In solace, we find all that we must know.

Refounding My Sacred Self

In echoes deep, the past begins to rise,
A sacred journey searching for the wise.
With every step, a piece of me restored,
In the heart's cocoon, my spirit soars.

I shed the layers that once bound my soul,
In the light of truth, I find my whole.
Refounding self, I weave the threads anew,
In sacred patterns, life's tapestry grew.

Each breath reflects the beauty of my quest,
In whispers soft, the universe attest.
Through trials faced, my spirit finds its song,
In unity with love, where I belong.

The mirror of the heart reveals my face,
In every flaw, a mark of divine grace.
Refounding what was lost, I now embrace,
The sacred path, my journey's true embrace.

With feet upon the ground, I find my place,
In every heartbeat, echoes of His grace.
Refounding self, in love I've become free,
In sacred stillness, I can truly see.

The Pool of Celestial Waters

Beneath the veil of stars, a pool of light,
Reflecting all the dreams that take their flight.
With each soft ripple, stories start to weave,
In celestial waters, hearts believe.

The moon dips low, a mirror in the night,
Inviting souls to dance in pure delight.
With open hands, I gather whispers rare,
In this sacred space, love fills the air.

The waters hold the secrets of the wise,
In stillness deep, I gaze among the skies.
A communion in the depths, I find my part,
In the pool of life, I know my heart.

Reflections of the past, like stars aglow,
Each shimmer speaks of journeys yet untold.
In celestial waters, dreams converge,
With faith as my anchor, I will emerge.

At dawn's first light, the waters shine anew,
A testament to all that I hold true.
In the pool of celestial love, I dwell,
Where spirit flows, and all the heart can tell.

A Symphony of Wholeness

In harmony, the heart shall sing,
A unity of souls in spring.
Where blessings flow like rivers wide,
In the embrace of love, abide.

With every note, a prayer ascends,
Together, we find how true love mends.
In melodies of grace, we rise,
With open arms toward the skies.

The breath of life, a sacred sound,
In every clash, beauty is found.
Our voices join, a vibrant call,
In faith and hope, we shall not fall.

Let every whisper echo clear,
A testament for all to hear.
In perfect tune, we praise the day,
For wholeness blossoms in this way.

With every beat, our spirits soar,
In the symphony, forevermore.
In this divine embrace, we see,
The path to love and harmony.

Beneath the Arc of Faith

Under the sky, where shadows play,
A gentle light guides the way.
In the silence, hear the call,
Beneath the arc, we rise and fall.

Each moment glimmers, truth unveiled,
In every heart, the spirit hailed.
With open eyes, we seek the dawn,
In many paths, we journey on.

The whispers of the sacred blend,
In unity, our hearts we send.
With tender hands, the bonds we weave,
In faith's embrace, we shall believe.

Together, we stand, spirits aligned,
In the arc of faith, love defined.
With every hope, we walk as one,
In sacred circles, we've begun.

Beneath the stars, our dreams take flight,
In every step, we find the light.
In timeless grace, our souls unite,
Beneath the arc, we share the light.

Mending the Broken Vessel

In shards of heart, where sorrow lay,
Hope finds a way to heal the fray.
With gentle hands, the pieces mold,
Each crack a story, brave and bold.

The blessing found in brokenness,
In every tear, a soft caress.
With patience grand, we gather round,
In love's embrace, new strength is found.

A vessel mended is full of grace,
In every flaw, the light we trace.
With hearts entwined, we learn to see,
In unity, we set them free.

Through trials faced, the spirit grows,
In every wound, compassion flows.
Together strong, we rise again,
In love's own hands, the journey begins.

In every heart, a sacred space,
The broken vessel finds its place.
From fragments lost, a blessing streams,
In mending, we fulfill our dreams.

The Light of the Infinite

In quiet moments, grace unfolds,
The light of love, a story told.
In every dawn, a new design,
The infinite shines, our hearts align.

With every breath, the spirit stirs,
In whispered truths, the journey occurs.
From shadows cast, we seek the flame,
In unity, we rise, the same.

The stars above, a guiding light,
In endless night, we find our sight.
With open hearts, we look within,
The light of truth, it draws us in.

Through trials faced and paths obscure,
In faith upheld, we grow more sure.
With every step, the love we share,
The infinite waits, a presence rare.

In sacred bonds, we journey forth,
In light and love, we find our worth.
With gratitude, our spirits soar,
The light of the infinite evermore.

The Glimmer of Holiness

In the quiet morn of dawn,
The world awakens, soft and bright.
Nature sings her sacred song,
Each note a glimmer of pure light.

Upon the earth, a tapestry,
Of colors vast and beauty rare.
In every leaf and every tree,
The whispers of holiness fill the air.

From mountain peaks to oceans wide,
The Spirit dances, ever near.
In each heartbeat, a gentle guide,
In every laugh, the joy is clear.

In fellowship with all we see,
United in love, we find our way.
In reverence, we bend the knee,
Embracing the gift of every day.

So let us share the glimmer bright,
A beacon shining through the strife.
Together, we will spread the light,
In the glimmer of holiness, our life.

Whispers from the Infinite

In the silence of the night's embrace,
Whispers call from realms beyond.
Soft songs echo through time and space,
Infinite love, forever fond.

With every breath, we hear the truth,
In rustling leaves and flowing streams.
The essence of faith, the gift of youth,
In quiet moments, we chase our dreams.

From starry skies to ocean deep,
Wisdom flows like rivers wide.
In sacred silence, secrets keep,
As we walk with the Divine as guide.

Let hearts awaken to love's sweet grace,
In every face, a spark divine.
In unity, we find our place,
In whispers soft, our spirits shine.

Embrace the sacred, let go of fear,
For in the infinite, we are whole.
With each whisper, let truth draw near,
In the light of love, we find our soul.

The Shattered Chalice

In shadows deep, a chalice lay,
Once a vessel, now in dismay.
Cracked and broken, yet still it gleams,
Reflecting the light of forgotten dreams.

Whispers of hope in the shards reside,
Promise of grace that will not subside.
From pieces small, a story unfolds,
Of faith revived and courage bold.

Raise it high, though it feels so frail,
In unity, we shall not fail.
Each fragment holds a sacred part,
Together they form a timeless heart.

Let its beauty be redefined,
In brokenness, our paths aligned.
For in the ruins, we find our song,
A melody deep where we belong.

Though shattered, our spirits rise anew,
Finding power in what we renew.
In every crack, a light shines through,
The shattered chalice, forever true.

Illumination Amidst the Fragments

In the darkness where shadows creep,
Fragments of light begin to leap.
Scattered pieces tell a tale,
Of lost journeys on a sacred trail.

Each broken shard, a glimpse of grace,
Illuminating the sacred space.
From chaos, beauty starts to form,
A guiding star in a raging storm.

Gathered here, we stand as one,
In fractures bright, our hope begun.
Together we weave a radiant thread,
With love and light, we shall be led.

The dance of faith amid despair,
In shattered moments, we find our prayer.
Each fragment whispers stories old,
Of spirits brave, of hearts bold.

Illumination amidst the night,
A symphony of the lost and bright.
Let us embrace the fractured light,
And find our way through sacred sight.

Sacred Mending of a Wandering Heart

In silence, whispers guide the way,
Healing hands where shadows lay.
Each breath a prayer, a gentle plea,
To find the love that sets us free.

With every tear, a treasure found,
Lost souls gather on sacred ground.
The heart's embrace, a warm refrain,
In unity, we break the chain.

Through valleys deep and mountains high,
We seek the light that will not die.
In sacred mending, hope is spun,
A journey starts, two hearts as one.

Upon the altar of the soul,
We weave our dreams, we find the whole.
With faith, our spirits intertwine,
In love's embrace, we see the sign.

So let us dance in holy fire,
In every heart, a sweet desire.
With open arms, the world we greet,
In sacred mending, life is sweet.

The Unraveling of Holy Threads

In quiet spaces, threads unfold,
A tapestry of stories told.
Each strand a lesson, rich and rare,
In woven paths, we find our share.

As shadows linger, light breaks through,
A dance of faith, in love anew.
The holy weave, both strong and frail,
In every stitch, the vows prevail.

With every fray, a chance to grow,
To understand what we don't know.
In sacred hands, the fibers part,
The unraveling, a work of art.

With patience, wisdom finds its way,
In crafted knots, we humbly pray.
Through trials faced and battles fought,
The holy threads connect our thoughts.

So gather close, dear souls in grace,
Embrace the journey, find your place.
In unity, our spirits rise,
The unraveling unveils the skies.

Pathways to the Rejoined Spirit

On twisting trails where shadows lie,
We walk in faith, our heads held high.
Each step an echo of love's decree,
Pathways formed where souls are free.

In morning light, the journey calls,
With every breath, the spirit sprawls.
In whispered winds, a sacred vow,
To follow truth, to live in now.

Beneath the stars, the heart takes flight,
In sacred dreams, we find the light.
The rejoined spirit, bright and bold,
In love's embrace, a tale retold.

Through winding roads, where shadows roam,
Our souls unite, we find our home.
In every heartbeat, a gentle guide,
The pathways lead where love abides.

So journey forth, dear heart, be still,
In every moment, find your will.
The pathways weave a sacred chart,
To guide the way of the rejoined heart.

From Ashes to Garden Blossoms

In fields of ashes, hope takes root,
With tender care, the seeds commute.
From pain's embrace, the blossoms rise,
In vibrant hues, they touch the skies.

Through trials faced and burdens borne,
The garden of renewal is worn.
Each flower blooming tells a tale,
Of strength in spirit that won't fail.

With gentle hands, we tend the earth,
In every loss, we find rebirth.
From ashes cold, the warmth ignites,
In hearts awakened, dreams take flight.

So plant the seeds of love and grace,
In every corner, find your space.
From ashes rise, let joy abound,
In gardens lush, our hope is found.

In unity, our spirits dance,
Beneath the sun, we take a chance.
From ashes bloom the sweetest song,
In garden blossoms, we belong.

Milton Keynes UK
Ingram Content Group UK Ltd.
UKHW020042271124
451585UK00012B/1011